CW01309945

Copyright: © Daniel Turner

SIMPLE HISTORY

ISBN-13: 978-1533660282

ISBN-10: 153366028X

All rights reserved. No part of this publication may be reproduced, stored in or introduced into a retrieval system, or transmitted in any form or by any means (electronic, mechanical, by photocopying, recording or otherwise) without the prior written permission of the author.

Part of the Simple guide series

Some images credited: freepik

Written by Daniel Turner & Tabitha Buckley

Illustrator:
Daniel Turner

This title is in United States English.

SIMPLE HISTORY

A SIMPLE GUIDE TO

THE AMERICAN CIVIL WAR

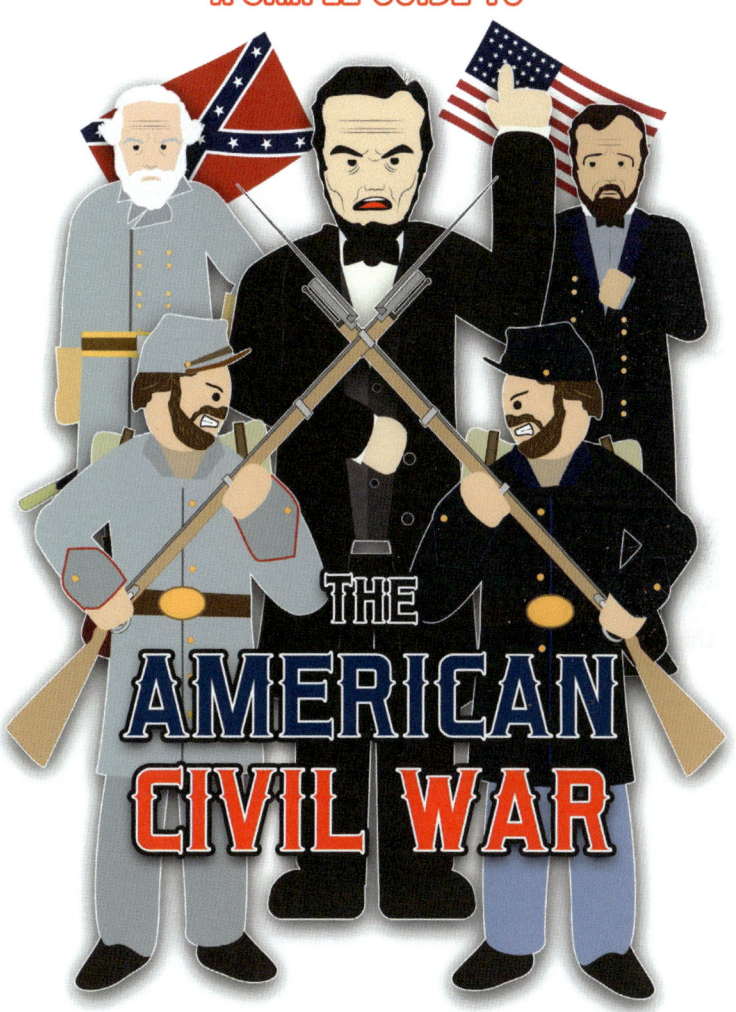

Written by Daniel Turner & Tabitha Buckley
Illustrated by Daniel Turner

Contents

Introduction — 5

TIMELINE

Slavery in America — 6

Lincoln's Election and the Confederate Constitution — 8

The Battle of Fort Sumter — 10

The Formation of the Union Army — 12

The First Battle of Bull Run — 13

Monitor vs. Merrimack — 14

The Battle of Shiloh — 16

The Battle of Antietam — 17

The Emancipation Proclamation — 18

The Battle of Gettysburg — 20

The Draft Riots — 22

Sherman's March to the Sea — 23

General Lee's Surrender — 24

Abraham Lincoln's Assassination — 25

The 13th Amendment — 26

THE WAR EXPERIENCE

28 — The Presidents

30 — The Generals

32 — The Soldiers

34 — Weapons and Equipment

36 — Photography in the Civil War

37 — The War By Numbers

INTRODUCTION

The American Civil War is one of America's most important historical moments. While the American Revolution established the United States of America, it was the Civil War of 1861-1865 which decided what type of country it would become. This war answered two important questions which still remained after the American Revolution:

Would the United States of America be a dissolvable collection of self-ruling states, or would the country exist as one powerful nation under a single president?

And would the country stand by the declaration that all men were created equal, or would it continue to rely on slavery as its main source of labor?

SLAVERY IN AMERICA

Slavery began in America in 1619. Over the space of 200 years, about 600,000 slaves were brought to the United States, most of whom were forced to work in cotton and tobacco plantations.

The slaves came from Africa, where they were packed tightly and chained up in slave ships to be brought to the American colonies. These vessels were rife with disease and starvation, so many slaves lost their lives simply on the voyage there.

Slaves had very few rights. They were not allowed weapons or to raise their hand against a white person, and they were never allowed to leave the plantation unless they were sold. Beatings were also, very common.

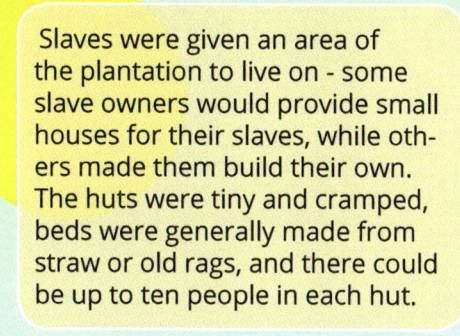

Slaves were given an area of the plantation to live on - some slave owners would provide small houses for their slaves, while others made them build their own. The huts were tiny and cramped, beds were generally made from straw or old rags, and there could be up to ten people in each hut.

Slaves were made to work from sunrise to sunset, and how many days off they got depended completely on their owner. Some slaves got one day off every month, others got to relax every Sunday. Some slaves got no free days at all, and had to work every day of the year.

Lincoln's Election and the Confederate Constitution 1860

Abraham Lincoln became the 16th President of the United States of America in 1860, causing seven of the Southern states to withdraw from the union due to his strong anti-slavery views. In 1861, these countries met to form the government of the Confederate States of America, consisting of Alabama, Florida, Georgia, Louisiana, Mississippi, South Carolina and Texas. The Confederacy's first president was Jefferson Davis.

Lincoln deemed this move illegal, but refused to act against it in a bid to avoid further conflict.

Many in the North supported this decision, as it placed responsibility for any future violence on the shoulders of the South.

The Battle of Fort Sumter
April 1861

Unlike Abraham Lincoln, Jefferson Davis announced in his first speech that the South would be willing to achieve its goals by using force. This happened that spring, in the Battle of Fort Sumter.

On the 12th of April, 1861, the South Carolinian military under the command of General P. T. Beauregard attacked Fort Sumter, a sea fort in South Carolina, which was occupied by the Union. After a day of heavy bombardment, the fort was surrendered to Beauregard's army by Major Robert Anderson and the Union forces. This victory, on the part of the confederacy, encouraged Arkansas, North Carolina, Tennessee, and Virginia to also secede from the Union.

These were the first shots of the Civil War.

The Formation of the Union Army

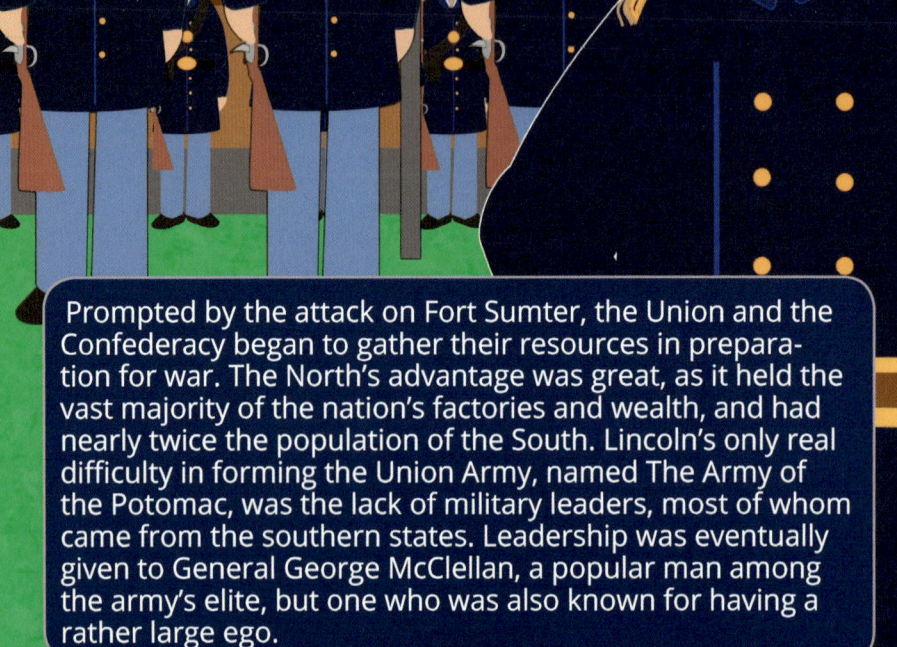

Prompted by the attack on Fort Sumter, the Union and the Confederacy began to gather their resources in preparation for war. The North's advantage was great, as it held the vast majority of the nation's factories and wealth, and had nearly twice the population of the South. Lincoln's only real difficulty in forming the Union Army, named The Army of the Potomac, was the lack of military leaders, most of whom came from the southern states. Leadership was eventually given to General George McClellan, a popular man among the army's elite, but one who was also known for having a rather large ego.

The First Battle of Bull Run
July 1861

It took time for the two armies to mobilize , the next battle was not fought until July, three months after the attack on Fort Sumter. Underestimating the gravity of the war, spectators came from both sides to watch the battle, some even packing picnics.

The Confederacy won the battle, and saw the easy victory as proof that they would win the war early. The Union forces, shocked out of indifference by their loss, realized that they needed to take their preparations more seriously if they were to have any hope of winning.

Monitor vs. Merrimack
March 1862

While the Union and Confederate armies clashed on land, their navies continued the struggle for control out at sea. Though the Confederate navy was much smaller than that of the North, the two sides turned out to be fairly evenly matched.

The Union had no choice but to build their own ironclad named the USS Monitor, which added a powerful gun turret. The two ships finally faced each other in the Battle of the Ironclads in March 1862, a battle which ended in a draw.

14

Refitting an old warship named the USS Merrimack with iron plates and a steam engine, the South built an important new naval weapon known as the ironclad, which could destroy Union ships with very little effort.

15

The Battle of Shiloh
April 1862

The Battle of Shiloh was an incredibly bloody engagement between the Confederate forces and the Union forces, led by General Ulysses S. Grant. This battle saw tens of thousands of men lose their lives. This time, Grant and the Union forces were victorious, proving to the Confederates that the war had not yet been won, and that Lincoln was serious about preserving the Union. It was the South's turn to face the bitter realities of a long, bloody war..

The Battle of Antietam
September 1862

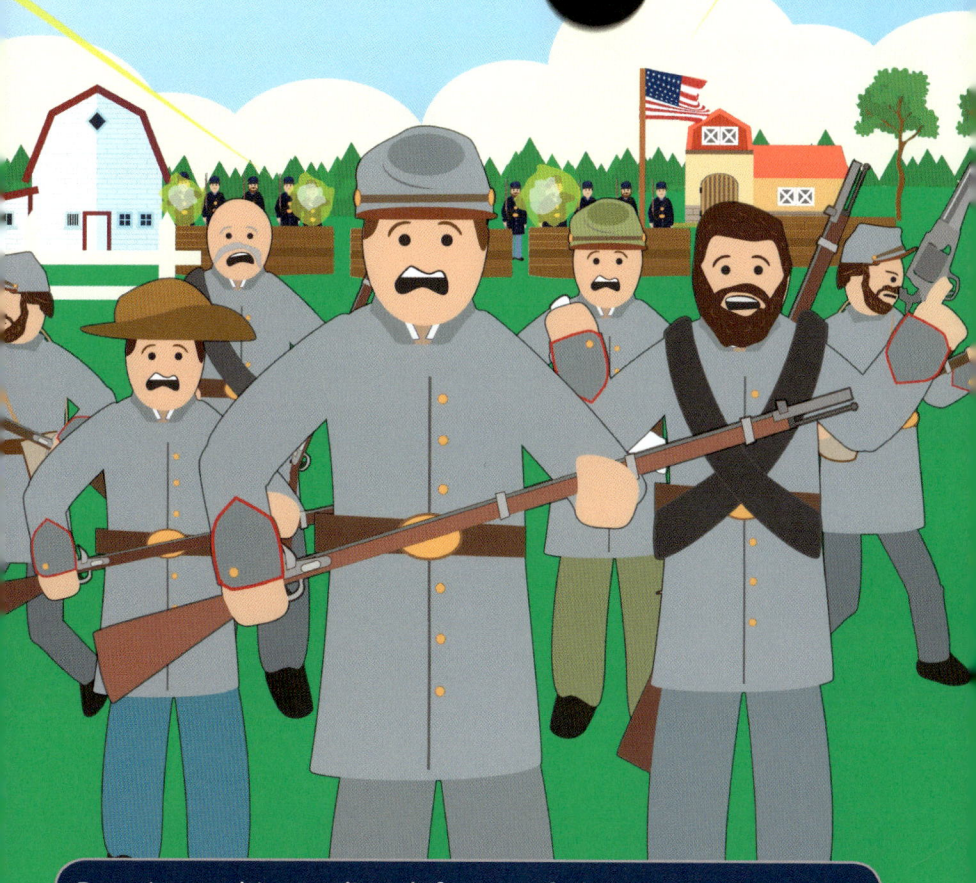

Reacting to this startling defeat, confederate General Robert E. Lee decided to press on into the border states and beat the Union on their own ground, believing that a victory in Maryland would cause the state to join the Confederacy. This plan failed in September 1862. Lee's troops faced the Union army at the Battle of Antietam, and were forced to retreat. This was the bloodiest day of the war, with more than 23,000 casualties.

The Emancipation Proclamation

After this victory, Lincoln decided to issue the Emancipation Proclamation, freeing all of the slaves in the Confederacy. This proclamation had a relatively minor effect, since it freed only those slaves in the Confederate states and not those in the border states, but it did highlight the fact that America could not exist as a single, powerful nation if slavery was allowed to continue.

JANUARY 1, 1863

19

The Battle of Gettysburg
July 1863

Refusing to be put-off by defeat, Lee and his troops marched into the Northern territory of Pennsylvania. There, his army fought the Union forces in the Battle of Gettysburg, a violent three-day long battle, in which more than 50,000 soldiers were killed. Once again, the Union forces were victorious, and the Confederates were repelled.

Neither General Meade nor General Lee were aware of the battle they were about to undertake, as it began without either of their permission.

63 Medals of Honor were awarded to Union soldiers for their service in the Battle of Gettysburg.

More than a third of all photos we have of dead soldiers from the Civil War come from this battle.

The Battle of Gettysburg proved to the North that the Confederates could be beaten and, more importantly, boosted their morale.

21

The Draft Riots
1863

In a bid to strengthen the Union army, Congress passed a new law demanding all young men to either join the army or donate $300 to the war effort. This meant that poorer men were forced to serve in the army, while richer men had a way of avoiding the draft.

NO DRAFT

Shocked by how unfair this new law was, many Northerners began to protest, and riots broke out across the nation. The worst riot took place in New York City, with poorer white men looting and burning large areas of the city. By the time the riots ended, more than 100 people had died.

Sherman's March to the Sea 1864

President Lincoln and General Grant understood that the war would have to end quickly if they were to restore the Union. They decided that they needed to increase their efforts, so General William Tecumseh Sherman was ordered to begin a march through the American Deep South. In the summer of 1864, General Sherman began his so called "March to the Sea".

The first stop on this march was Atlanta, where Sherman defeated the Confederate troops and captured the city. The citizens of Atlanta refused to surrender to the Union, so Sherman burned the city to the ground and continued his march.

Sherman's March caused massive amounts of damage and destruction before he finally reached Savannah in December. The city quickly surrendered, allowing Sherman to capture the important port city and end his March to the Sea.

GENERAL LEE'S SURRENDER
APRIL 1865

Breaking through Robert E. Lee's defenses in April 1865, General Grant forced the Confederate forces to retreat for the last time. As a final gesture of defiance, the Confederates burned Richmond, once their own capital city, so that the Union forces could not use it.

After years of fighting, General Lee realized that he had been overpowered, and that his men were malnourished and unfit for duty. Rather than fighting on until their inevitable defeat, Lee formally surrendered to Grant at the Appomattox Courthouse in Virginia on April 9, 1865.

With Lee's surrender and the capture of the other Confederate Generals, the Civil War had finally come to an end.

Abraham Lincoln's Assassination
April 1865

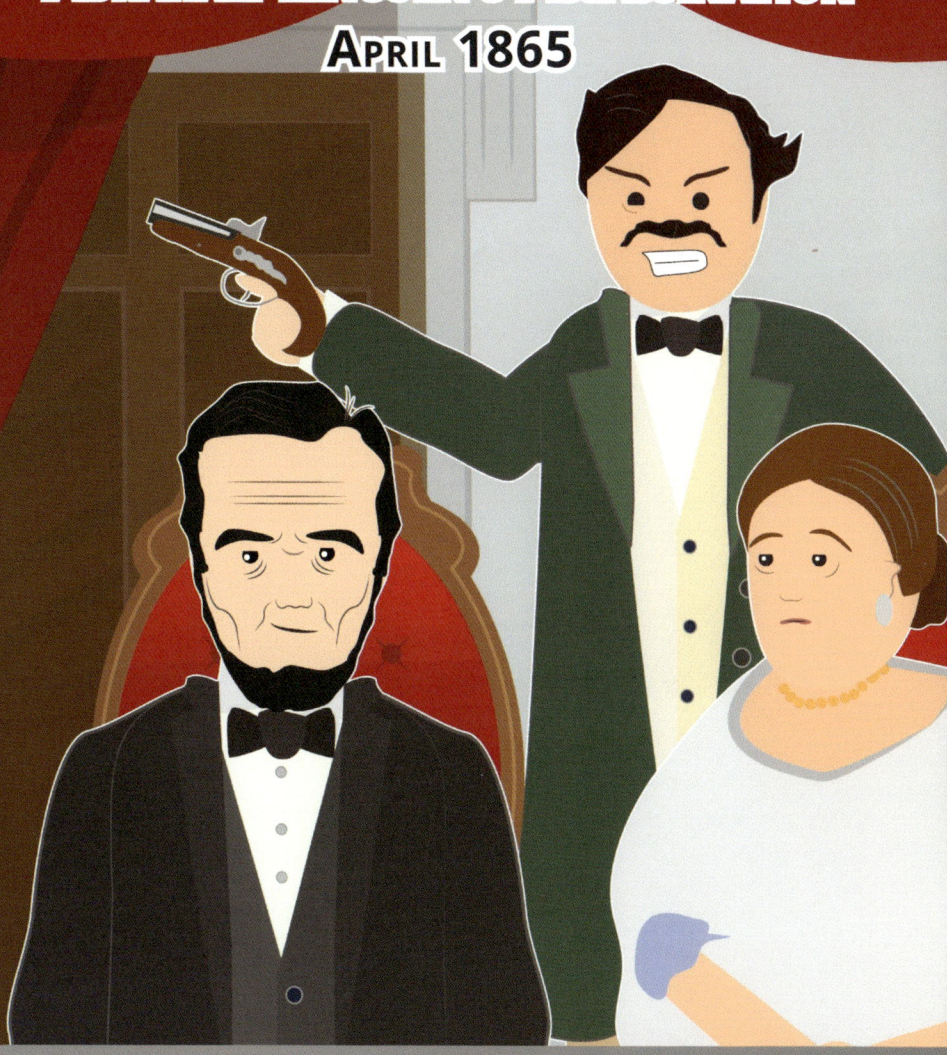

Just 5 days after General Lee's surrender, on April 14, 1865, John Wilkes Booth shot President Abraham Lincoln as he watched a Play at Ford's Theatre in Washington, D.C. The murder was a final attempt at saving the Confederacy by throwing the government into confusion.

The 13th Amendment
December 1865

The 13th Amendment entered the United States Constitution on December 6th, 1865, finally finishing what President Lincoln started with the Emancipation Proclamation. This amendment abolished slavery in the entire United States of America.

THE WAR EXPERIENCE

THE PRESIDENTS
ABRAHAM LINCOLN

Once a lawyer in Illinois, Abraham Lincoln was the sixteenth president of the United States, a man whose strong beliefs meant his election prompted the beginning of the Civil War. Lincoln aimed to keep the states together in a strong union and to free all slaves. Lincoln's goals were eventually reached but not before his death in 1865.

JEFFERSON DAVIS

Jefferson Davis was a senator from Mississippi who, in 1861, became the first president of the Confederacy in his attempt to unify all of the Southern states into a central government.

The Generals

Ulysses S. Grant

The top general in the Union during the Civil War, Ulysses S. Grant, later became the eighteenth president of the United States of America. Throughout the war, he fought mercilessly against the Confederates earning the nickname "Unconditional Surrender" Grant.

George McClellan

George McClellan was the general chosen to command the Union army when Robert E. Lee turned down the role. He had some victories, but was ultimately fired for being too cautious. McClellan attempted to stand against Lincoln in the 1864 election, but was defeated.

Robert E. Lee

Grant's main adversary, Robert E. Lee, turned down the chance to command the Union forces, choosing instead to command the Army of Northern Virginia on the Confederate side. Lee was the best General in the U.S. Army at the time, and supported the United States, but believed that it was his duty to fight for his native state, Virginia.

Lee surrendered to Grant unconditionally and ended the Civil War in 1865.

William Tecumseh Sherman

Ulysses S. Grant's friend and fellow Union general, William Tecumseh Sherman battled the Confederate forces relentlessly during his March to the Sea through the American Deep South.

The Soldiers

The Union Army

The Union Army fought in support of the Union and the abolition of slavery. The army included the soldiers of the permanent U.S. Army, but the vast majority were volunteers. Over 2 million men served in this army.

Union soldiers wore a blue uniform, made up of a black felt hat, Prussian blue coat, dark or sky blue greatcoat and sky blue trousers.

The Confederate States Army

Fighting for the Confederate States, the Confederate States Army fought to protect their freedom and their rights to own slaves. This army was made up of about 1 million soldiers, as well as an unknown amount of slaves who were forced to carry out various tasks for the army.

Confederate soldiers wore a gray uniform that varied greatly according to the cost and availability of materials, locations, state regulations and rank of the soldiers.

Weapons and Equipment

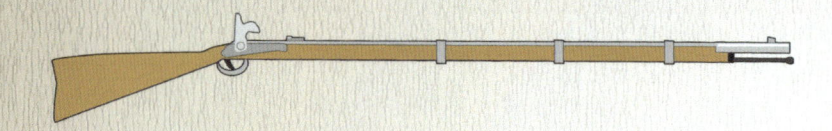

Springfield Model 1861

Rifles

The rifle most commonly used during the Civil War was the Springfield Model 1861 rifled musket. It was generally used for more long-range fighting, preferred in battle for its reliability, accuracy and range.

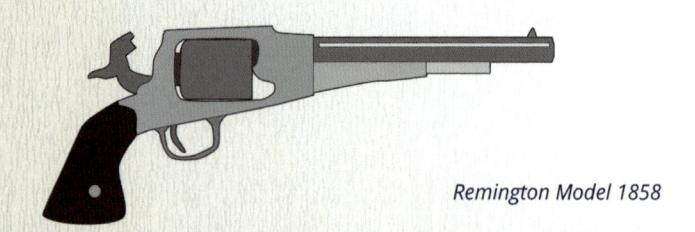

Remington Model 1858

Handguns

Small handguns such as pistols and revolvers were used by many soldiers as a backup in case of close-quarters fighting. The most commonly used brands were Colt and their main competitor Remington, though there was no one standardized weapon.

SWORDS

Edged weapons were carried by both sides during the Civil War. The most popular sword carried by officers was the Model 1850 Army Staff and Field Officer's Sword.

Model 1850 Army Staff and Field Officer's Sword

EQUIPMENT

As well as his weapons, the average soldier during the Civil War would carry a canteen and a knapsack containing his personal belongings such as tobacco, letters, cards, and eating utensils.

Photography in the Civil War

Although the American Civil War was not the first war to have been photographed, it was the first to have been photographed extensively. Brave photographers would even enter the battlefields to capture the war up close, and their photographs were displayed and sold throughout the country.

The cameras used at that time were very different from the ones we use today. The technique used at the time was "wet-plate photography": the photographed image was captured on a plate of glass coated in chemicals. The process was very complicated, especially when carried out on the battlefield.

The War in Numbers

11 Seceded States

South Carolina, Mississippi, Florida, Alabama, Georgia, Louisiana, Texas, Virginia, Arkansas, North Carolina, and Tennessee

Four Years

Fought by 2,128,948 Union Soldiers at $13 per month

and

1,082,119 Confederate Soldiers at $11 per month,

with 1522 Medals of Honor

and up to 850,000 deaths.

50 Major Battles

and over 5,000 minor battles resulting in

3.9 million freed slaves

and

1 United Nation

Simple Guides

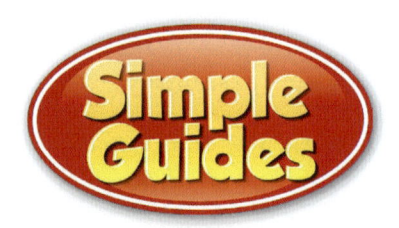

Available now & coming soon!

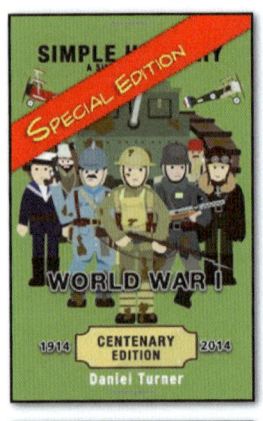

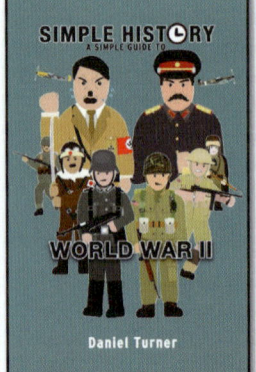

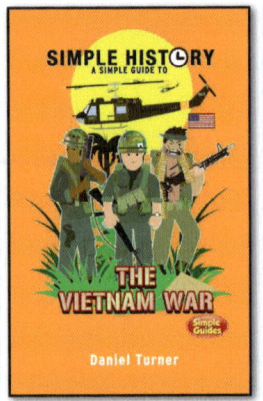

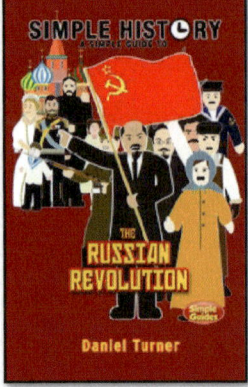

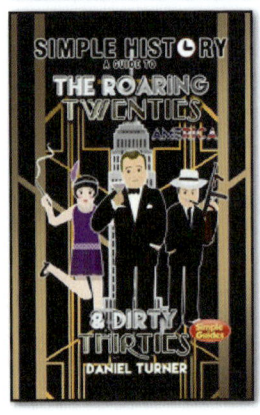

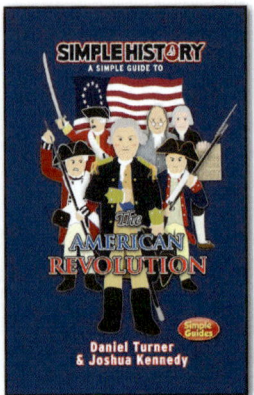

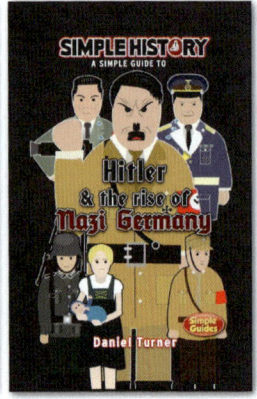

- Simple History: A Simple Guide to World War I — Special Edition, Centenary Edition 1914–2014 — Daniel Turner
- Simple History: A Simple Guide to World War II — Daniel Turner
- Simple History: A Simple Guide to Henry VIII — Daniel Turner
- Simple History: A Simple Guide to The Space Race — Daniel Turner
- Simple History: A Simple Guide to The Vietnam War — Daniel Turner
- Simple History: A Simple Guide to The Russian Revolution — Daniel Turner
- Simple History: A Guide to The Roaring Twenties & Dirty Thirties — Daniel Turner
- Simple History: A Simple Guide to The American Revolution — Daniel Turner & Joshua Kennedy
- Simple History: A Simple Guide to Hitler & the rise of Nazi Germany — Daniel Turner

On tablet / phone   **computer**   **print**

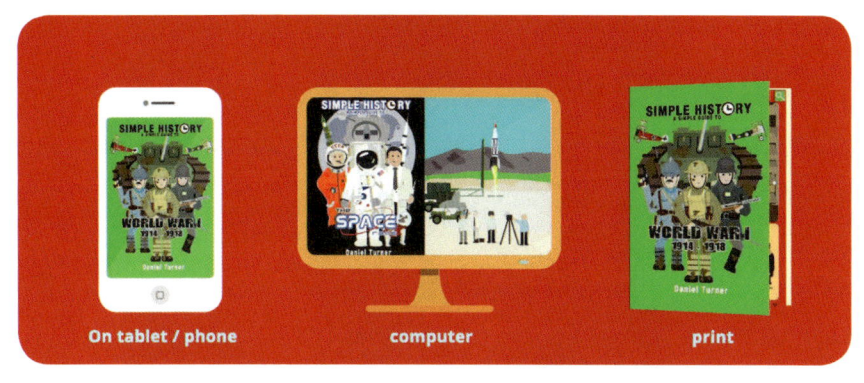

In print, tablet and e-book formats

Sign up for the mailing list for Simple History news. Simply Scan the QR code to the left with your phone.

Visit the website and social media!

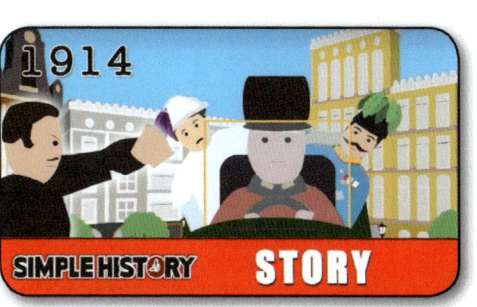

www.simplehistory.co.uk

Printed in Great Britain
by Amazon